THE TRUE INTERPRETATION OF DREAMS

The Hidden Truth About Dreams

Cadet Mwankana

ACKNOWLEDGEMENTS

Thank you to myself. I am the only one that I have.

In memory of my great friend and brother, Alain Lussambo. What a great legacy you have left me! R.I.P.

To the great master "Muni" Michael Weber, thank you with all my heart. Without you I would still be blind today.

To my friend, Susanna Ding.
Do you see the irony? Me, who doesn't like to read.
I have never forgotten that conversation with you.
You're the greatest woman!

CONTENTS

"Through meditation one has to achieve a dreamless sleep with full alertness. Once this happens, the drop falls into the ocean and becomes the ocean "

Rajneesh

Prologue

What I am going to offer you here is a tool that you can put into practice, that you can use day after day, night after night to develop your exploration of the self, of the understanding of oneself, so as to overcome your deepest fears, which will lead to peace, to joy, to the growth of your being.

No, I am not going to offer you more knowledge to embellish your intellect. I am not going to provide you with extra information to enrich the fantasies of your mind and plunge you into new dream-like adventures.

What I am going to present you with here is very simple and sometimes dull. The mind does not like simplicity. The mind likes mystery, it likes that which it does not entirely understand, what escapes it. Yet truth is always simple. It is always present, always now. Never elsewhere, never before, never after. Truth is always there, right in front of you, ready to be grasped. But naturally, the mind complicates the truth to avoid it. I will therefore be very straightforward, very concise, and brutally honest. I will follow the path of simplicity and frankness.

In this book I am going to offer you a tool, to provide you with a new way to understand your dreams which will help you to put into practise the spiritual teachings about self-awareness, a way to live each day in the present moment, in accordance with the truth. Besides, as the Bible says, it is only by knowing the truth that the truth will set you free (John 8:32).

With practice, you will dream less and less until you rarely dream at all. What freedom! For you sleep neither deeply nor calmly when you dream. You do not rest properly. I will tell you what the greatest benefit is to dreaming less: inner peace. The less dreams you have, the more you find inner peace. The two go hand in hand.
This work is intended for anyone who has dreams at night whilst sleeping. Dreams have a tremendous influence on us. We are all aware of this. Sometimes dreams terrify us, sometimes they fill us with happiness for a short while, and sometimes they give us hope. I say 'hope' and not that they lead us to have expectations, because expectation is something you will gain when you understand how to handle your dreams and how to interpret them for the best possible development of your entire being.

WHAT EXACTLY IS A DREAM?

Dream and Thought

Without looking in a dictionary, everyone knows what a dream is: images we see whilst sleeping and often remember upon waking up. Everyone dreams, it's true. There are some people who dream more often than others. But there are also some who only dream on rare occasions: once a week or once a month, or even once a year. And there are even some who do not dream at all.

I am going to give you another definition of what a dream is, a second explanation that will help us more than the first mentioned above, and that will help us far more than the definition extracted from a dictionary: Dreams are nothing other than thought. Yes, those "images that we see whilst sleeping and often remember upon waking up" are just another way of thinking.

How is it that thoughts arise within us? Upon closer inspection, we see that this phenomenon takes place as often as breathing. Therefore I would like to suggest a small experiment to you:

Close your eyes for a minute and observe the darkness before you. Thoughts are going to appear in your mind. Whether you want them to or not, thoughts will come and go, one following on from another. When you have finished this exercise you will notice that your thoughts appear in different forms: they can be images, sounds, voices, words, entire scenarios and in some instances conceptual thoughts.

Thought is in itself neither good nor bad, neither stupid nor great, neither positive nor negative. Thoughts are simply there. They appear and disappear, one after the other.

In truth, thoughts have no relation to one another. It is the mind that forms the connections according to the impressions that it has accumulated since the beginning of its existence. This is the lie of the mind. It is not without reason that the Bible calls it 'the devil', the liar, the seducer.

I am going to illustrate a typical lie of the mind: I have a friend in the Congo who, at the age of three years old, had a brother. For the first three years of his life before the arrival of this brother, he had been the favourite child of his mother. In other words, he only knew this: from morning until night, all of his mother's attention was focused on him. He also had an older sister who was ten years old, but the age difference between the two siblings was large enough for my friend not to consider his older sister to be a rival for his mother's attention. Therefore, the boy enjoyed the attention that his mother gave him alone. The mother did not work and dedicated her life to taking care of her two children. This little three-year-old child had/felt/experienced deep love for his mother. For that matter, the love that one experiences at this young age is the same deep love that a man looks for in a woman as an adult. For a female, it is the love between herself and her father. You now know that if you want to understand how you love in your romantic relationships as an adult, whether you're male or female, it is important to try to understand your love for your mother during your childhood, or for your father if you are female.

In any case, this little boy was the youngest of the family and everyone cherished him. But his life changed the day his mother returned from the hospital with a new-born baby in her arms. Shocked, his world then collapsed: he no longer recognised his mother, to him, his mother had changed. The mother was of course the same, but for this young boy, the expression on his mother's face, the gentle look she had for the new baby, was terrifying for him. From that moment on, he knew he had lost his mother, his true love. She had abandoned him for another. This thought remained

engraved in his mind, and all the events which followed only reinforced this thought in the form of law: "true love never lasts", "sooner or later she will leave you for somebody else". These two laws established themselves as the days went by with the new baby always in the mother's arms and all the rest of the family coming to pamper the infant. A vision of horror for our little boy.
As an adult, whenever he has feelings for a woman, he knows deep down that it will not last, that she will leave him some day for somebody else. The worst part is that these two mental rules do not only apply to women, but to all relationships in which he establishes emotional bonds.

This could be his dog, his partner, his best friend, or anyone else. But all romantic relationships are especially influenced by these rules. When he separates from a partner for example, he says to himself "I knew it, … they always leave anyway!". It is important to note however that there is no connection between his relationship with a woman and his experience with his mother at three years old. No connection at all. Yet the mind creates a link, perhaps even several, and it judges, prejudges, hopes, controls, watches and accuses. And when the mind creates these connections, it also provides arguments to justify them. This is the lie. These arguments

are only pretexts. And as we all know, the mind is very talented at this game.
This example was simple, but these types of lies do exist in reality only much more complex, and they appear all the time whenever we think. It is the practise of those who have committed themselves to any of the so-called 'spiritual' approaches to catch these lies of the mind in the act.

The mind is nothing other than a liar. Etymological dictionaries demonstrate this well: in French for example, the word 'mental' meaning 'mind' stems from the Latin term 'mens' which signifies 'mind, spirit, thinking principle, activity of thought, intelligence'. According to Jean-Claude Rolland, in his book 'Les grandes familles de mots', this Latin word 'mens' and the verb 'mentiri' (in French: 'mentir') are directly linked and are the ancestors of a whole family of words that derive from it. This is the case with all French words with -ment-, -mens-, and -mence, in them such as: mental, menteur, mention, mentir, comment, commentaire, dément, démenti, démentir, mensonge, mensonger, démence, véhémence ». You can trace this link in the following French words in regard to their 'men-' stem: 'Mental' (mind), 'mentir' (to lie), 'songe' (dream), 'mensonge' (lie). Thus, as the French words and their Latin roots demonstrate, the mind and the dream are closely linked and share a common ancestor: le 'mensonge' (the lie).

The Mind

The mind is a sophisticated machine that has only one function: to accumulate information, store it, organise it according to a particular logic and provide us with the information when needed. This system is comparable to Google, one of the biggest machines in the world. If you type a word into Google, it presents you with information which sometimes has a connection to the initial word.

The mind does exactly the same thing, even when we do not ask anything of it. It works continuously without stopping. Thereby, the thoughts that our minds propose to us are not actually us, even if they appear in the form of the first person 'I'. This is just part of the information that we have accumulated since birth.

Thus the mind sends out thoughts that emerge in the field of consciousness and you become aware of them. The mental machine is always working; that's why it was created in the first place.

The field of consciousness is vaster than you perceive it to be, and the little exercise I proposed earlier of closing your eyes and contemplating the darkness before you helps you to directly experience this field of consciousness that is present. Whether our eyes are open or whether we are asleep, it is there. But the ordinary state of the human being experiences consciousness in its limited form, and not its unlimited form. We experience consciousness in its limited form through the identification of the self, of the sense of 'me', the 'ego'. It is this consciousness that makes me think of myself as 'me', and that which I do not identify as being part of myself, as 'you'. I am myself and therefore different to another, and thus duality arises. However, the masters of all the religious and so-called 'spiritual' traditions maintain that there is only 'One' but the mind makes 'two' out of it. As Jesus said, 'I and the father are one' (John 10:30).

It is not the intention here to develop the subject on thought or the meaning of the ego. We will speak of this on another occasion. I am only trying to make the link between 'thought' and 'dream' here.

What does the mind do when it experiences something? It is going to try to respond, to give us an appropriate answer, according to its judgement evidently. And the mind is going to search for a response in its database where it stores all that it has experienced since birth, all the conclusions it has drawn, all the judgements it has made, etc. This can all be found in our personal databases. The mind has made rules and formulas out of all the conclusions it has formed from our experiences since birth, devising laws which govern our lives from morning till night.

An excellent example is this: one day I was visited by an old friend. I had just come out of a break up and told my friend how my last relationship ended. My friend reacted by laughing: 'my dear, never underestimate a woman when it comes to grudges. A woman prepares her next move in silence, even if it's over years. And when she strikes, you're finished.' There you have it, two mental rules were well formed: 'never underestimate women…', and 'they prepare their next move…'. The mind has had experiences in the past, and from them it has drawn general conclusions which it has stored in the form of principles or as rules which are applied to all similar situations. When the mind experiences a somewhat similar situation again, it is going to draw from its database and pick the fitting piece of information. In regard to the aforementioned example, in reality the mind should instead state: 'sometimes it would be better not to underestimate women…', and 'women are capable of preparing their next move over a long period of time without a man noticing it'. This is a simple way of revealing how the mind functions. It improves the more we gain experience, just as how the algorithm of Google grows the more we use it. It is the same in the earlier example of the young three-year-old boy. Formulated correctly, his mind would have stated: 'sometimes true love doesn't last', or 'it can happen that she leaves you for another'. But obviously, at the age of three, this poor little boy was not able to understand his mother.

The mind makes connections so quickly that we do not even realise it happens. Worse still, it is not only that we do not realise it, but also that we believe that we ourselves are the ones doing it, that the voices that we hear are our own. Thus, the game is twice as distorted.

Yet you are not to blame in all of this. The mind acts on its own accord, and it goes about its own business when you are awake and when you are asleep. And while you're sleeping, the mind constantly produces thoughts. Not as many as when you are awake, but it does produce them. This is what we call dreams.

When you dream whilst sleeping, the mind makes connections between all the information that it has in its database. There is nothing created anew in a dream. Everything that appears in the dream comes from within us. The dream's story may appear to be new, but in reality it is not. No matter how extraordinary the dream may be, all the information in the dream comes from our experiences in the past. All the elements of a dream come from within you beforehand. The mind is just full of imagination and skilled enough to create links and represent them to us in the dream as though they were new elements.

When we are awake, we live on the one hand with the mind and on the other with consciousness. The mind works to deliver information to us that is stored in its database when we ask it to, such as when we reflect on something or try to remember something. Additionally, the mind also makes connections between pieces of information, even without us asking. Just try for a minute not to think of anything and you will see that thoughts continue to come to mind. Those who practise meditation are aware of this.

As for consciousness, it is the witness to the mind, being aware of all its activities. Both co-exist simultaneously. But for most human beings, the mind makes more of a noise – so much noise in fact that it obscures the presence of self-awareness. On the other hand, self-awareness does not disappear, it is just concealed as a result of all the other activities and noises of the mind. Often we do not hear it when it expresses itself. But when we do hear it, the noise of the mind is so loud that we confuse the two. Take intuition, for example. The majority of us don't even really know what intuition is. It is a word that we are familiar with, but without truly knowing what it signifies. Intuition is information that comes from the heart (or the gut if you will); in other words from our core, from the innermost regions of ourselves, where self-awareness lies. Intuition is the information that consciousness itself conveys to us concerning what is or what should be done.

This information given by consciousness is clear and is accompanied by a feeling of certainty, the sentiment of being 100% sure of something, even if we do not have reasons to explain or justify it in the moment. But even then, as long as the mind is cloudy, we are often going to doubt this information and generally we will not take it at face value and confuse it with thoughts. It is only with practise that we come to distinguish between 'intuition' and 'thought'. Other than intuition, self-awareness is also expressed through feelings such as the feeling of certainty and the feeling of fulfilment.

But anyway, let us return to the subject at hand. Since the mind makes so much noise, the expression of consciousness, for example of intuition, is drowned out in all the din of the mind. It is only when we progress far enough down the path of self-awareness, of becoming more self-aware, that we can distinguish between intuition and thought.

But when we sleep, the activity of the mind subsides, just as with meditating sitting or lying down. During this form of meditation, it often happens that one falls asleep. This is in fact because it puts us in a frame of mind in which the mind settles down. And when the mind subsides, self-awareness automatically has more space to express itself. This is a well-known phenomenon amongst those who practise seated meditation. And this phenomenon not only occurs during meditation, but also during sleep. As we gradually slip into a deep sleep, the mind and all its activities subside – though not completely.

Self-awareness takes advantage of this moment to reveal certain information to us by using parts of the mind such as the mind's database where the information is stored.

Where Do Dreams Come From?

Despite the technological progress of the 20th century, the world of dreams still remains uncharted territory in science. So far, scientific researchers have not succeeded in understanding much concerning dreams. Of course, how will they be able to understand dreams which belong to the realm of consciousness? There are some things that will always escape science, that's just the way it is. And even if some progress is made, it will only be partial. I will speak of this later on. For now, I know that science only has hypotheses which yield nothing of value for those seeking true happiness or those who want peace of heart.

'Our Western civilisation, dominated by intellect, considers dreams to be a negligible phenomenon. On the contrary, among so-called 'primitive' people, the superiority of dreams goes without saying. Everything is a question of perspective, of culture and tradition', states Christine Maillard in her book 'Le Rêve, Histoire et significations'.

Where do dreams come from? The spiritual masters attain such knowledge through experience or intuition. Let us trust in their knowledge and we will solve our biggest problems. It is as simple as that. Of course, for scientists the assertions of the sages are only nonsense. That is nothing new. But if you want to heal yourself, the sages are giving you a secret. You do not have to trust them. To know the truth, you just have to put it to the test: go, practise, and the results will be telling. That is all, there is nothing to debate. Just take action and verify for yourself. That's what I did and I have seen the result, and it is marvellous.

Dreams are a form of thought that appear to us at night when the mind is at rest. Our consciousness uses this gateway to show us certain truths that we are not able to see when the mind is in full operation.

When the sages tell us such a truth, we, as truth-seekers, have only one duty before us: to verify it. Verify it until we evolve ourselves, understand and bear witness to our own words. The more we progress along the path of self-awareness, the more we understand ourselves and our own inner workings. The more we understand ourselves, the better we understand one another. There is no need to study the other, for to study oneself is more than enough. And with time we will come to understand life. All the questions we have will disappear. Calmness settles in and emotions calm down.

Dreams In The Spiritual World

There are plenty of publications on the subject of dreams. But the majority of them will neither help you to develop in your thinking nor in your emotions. Most of them speak of attractive and tempting methods, but you are only going to lose time and get lost in minor detail. They will talk to you about incubation dreams, therapeutic dreams, premonitory dreams, astral projecting, lucid dreams…

From a spiritual point of view, there is only one type of dream. These distinctions are not so important. I stress from a spiritual point of view as this signifies from the perspective of practise on the path to self-awareness. Otherwise we fall into dogmas and theories which lead us nowhere either. This is what establishes the difference between spirituality and religion. In religion, we are asked to be satisfied with believing that God will do the rest. We have all seen where this has led us: inquisitions, Christianity, colonialism, black slavery, etc. The so-called spiritual paths ask us to practise the teachings to test if what the guru says is true. There is no place for belief, only verification. It is exactly the same for what I am proposing here regarding dreams.

I said that from a spiritual point of view, there is only one type of dream and that the distinctions that many make do not play a large role. There is always a main element to each dream that one can take so as to evolve oneself. The rest is but distractions, with definitions made out of them to embellish entire libraries, to create a whole world, a whole dream science, which many therapists will use to their advantage to make money. It's not bad, it's just business. Everything has its place. But this way of approaching dreams teaches us nothing on self-awareness. You will always carry your fears in you and you will never see the mind at work. This way of approaching dreams will keep you a prisoner in the interpretation of dreams, and under these conditions you will always have dreams and there will never be an end. Do you want to interpret dreams until the end of your life? I do not. I want to put and end to dreaming and sleep in peace in the tranquillity of the night.

There will always be something new to see in your dreams, always an adventure more exciting than the last, and the journey can always go further than it did before. But to what length? You will end up meeting in your dreams all the angels, genies and divine creatures that there are, whatever they may be, and peace of mind will not come with all that. As amazing as it can seem, no dream will bring you peace of mind, calmness or happiness. Even God himself could appear to you in a dream in all his splendour and reveal all that he can to you, but even this will not bring you peace of mind and you will continue to live your life carried away by childish emotions and judgement. 'Do not judge' orders the Bible (Matthew 7:1).

So why not use dreams to progress in the quest for happiness? We have a good opportunity: use dreams as a tool for self-awareness and, little by little, free ourselves of emotions and instead leave room for a sense of self…, and little by little, see the mind at work and uncover its lies one after another.

We are going to approach the subject of dreams in the light of spirituality. In other words, approach dreams in such a way that one can practise using the dream to reach a certain state of mind which will be permanent. To approach dreams in the light of putting into practise the spiritual teaching received, whatever it may be.

HOW TO INTERPRET DREAMS

To Be Carried Away By Emotions

In this chapter we will talk about the mechanism that takes place a few hours before sleep. Dreams are not there just to show us amazing creatures or to let us experience wonderful adventures. No, there's a lot that takes place beforehand. To start with, it is necessary to note that our consciousness is awake 24 hours a day, even in the deepest part of our sleep. It retains everything and knows everything. It is 'witness' to the events in our lives, although we are often not aware of it because of the large influence of the mind on our spirit. It is so strong that we spend a large part of our days 'identified' with thoughts and 'carried away' by emotions in such a way that we do not 'see' the key events that affect us and cause emotions to arise. And out of these events that affect us, our consciousness chooses one or two to show us in a dream so that we are aware of them and are well advised for the next time. Let us briefly shed light on the terms that I have just used so that we speak the same language.

To 'See'

What does it mean to 'see' an emotion? Not seeing with the eyes, but with the heart. I am not speaking of the heart in regard to the term's meaning as an organ, as the term 'heart' also refers to the 'centre': at the heart of something. There is nothing deeper in us than our consciousness, and it can be found at the centre of our being. To see with the heart therefore signifies to be aware of something. When one speaks of the heart in a spiritual context, it is rather consciousness that is being considered. To have heartache, to love with all your heart, to take something to heart, the list goes on. All these examples allude to our profundity, to our deepest feeling, to the heart of us. Knowing that an emotion is there does not mean 'seeing' emotion, because knowing takes place on the level of the head, of the mind. To 'see' the emotion is just to be aware of it, to be conscious of it. It is nothing more than that.

It is in our childhood, from pregnancy until the age of 6 and even afterwards, where the majority of our adult traumas originated from. Why? Because children are not aware that they are able to be aware. An adult is able to be distracted, but when shown the technique, they can practise becoming more aware. A child cannot do this. They take everything in – even the faults of their irresponsible parents, absorbing them through lack of vigilance. To be conscious of what happens around us is not an easy task. Even adults do not manage to do this most of the time. I will speak more on this in the next chapter on lucidity.

To 'Be Identified With'

When you see a thought, it loses its power over you and it disappears. Then the next one rises and so on. But when you do not see a thought, when you are not aware of it, you automatically identify yourself with it. You believe that the thought is your voice. Therefore it becomes your identity, a part of you, or it even becomes you, according to your viewpoint. If the mind establishes a connection between this thought and a past event, a painful event for example, emotions will arise. There are strong emotions as well as others which do not affect us and pass unnoticed. It should also be remembered that there are of course thoughts that are not toxic and do not necessarily provoke emotions. But let us assume that an emotion arises in response to something. In that moment you also have the possibility of seeing the emotion, of becoming aware of it. If this is the case, the emotion is going to lose its power over you and will disappear. But if on the contrary you identify yourself with the emotion and dedicate a lot of energy to it, then it will grow.

This is why spiritual teachings speak of identification with the ego. This identification takes place on several levels. Consciousness identifies itself with thoughts and emotions and thereby limits itself to the sense of the individualised 'I'.

To 'Be Affected'

From the moment you identify yourself with either thought or emotion, both will affect you, collide with you. When you are affected by both, they can go so far as to leave a mark deep within you. The mind will save this imprint in its database to remember each time something similar happens. This is what happens in our childhood: the ego takes in so much and far too many events leave their mark in the child's mind, and as we grow, the rest of our lives are influenced by all these past marks.

To 'Be Carried Away'

To say that one is carried away by thoughts signifies that one identifies themself with them. It is the same for emotions. When emotions manifest they have a life span depending on their nature: they can last a second, a few minutes, even hours or weeks. Throughout this time, one remains identified with this emotion if an effort is not made to return to one's authentic self. This is what is called 'handling an emotion badly', or 'to badly come to terms with an event': the loss of oneself as a result of identifying with the mind and its thoughts and emotions. It does not matter if the emotion is negative or positive – even the joy of having won the lottery is an emotion that is subject to the same mechanisms as any other emotion. To free oneself of emotions signifies no longer having to feel them, whether they are agreeable or disagreeable, so as to leave space only for the sentiment of the heart.

And when one gets carried away with their thoughts or emotions, the 'Witness' is consequently no longer present. Yet when the 'Witness' awakens in us, even if only for two precious seconds, one is not carried away for these two seconds. We will speak of this later on.

When one knows all this, it becomes easy to understand the phenomenon of dreams and to glimpse its meaning.

Interpretation

How is it that dreams are to be understood? Muni, a German spiritual master, always told me that 'dreams are a manifestation of all that you have had bad experiences of a few hours before, and nothing else'. There you have it – everything is contained within these words. You can now close this book.

All the teaching is there in Muni's phrase: what you do not see when you are awake has an effect on you, and the conscious attempts to show you these things when the mind is at rest. There are certainly many things that we do not see, but the conscious cannot show us the thousands of things that we let slip during the day. There are two explanations for this. On the one hand, we would not know how to take in all this information. And on the other, in order to progress, it is better to take it step by step, one thing at a time. Thereby we only dream of one or two things that we did not take in the day before.

Everything that the conscious shows us in a dream will come back to us in the future; that is why it shows them to us in dreams. In this way, we will be better prepared the next time that we are faced with the same difficulty. Hence, if you interpret your dreams correctly, when these events return in the future you will be more astute and better prepared to handle them in that moment and thus overcome them.

Some will say that in order to interpret your dreams you have to keep a dream diary and write them down along with all possible details, even paying attention to every minor detail because each element of the dream may be hiding crucial information, a decisive clue that would be a key to decoding the dream. They will also say that the symbols especially should not be ignored because they are important, containing the history of an era and people, and that the symbol is a universal language…, etc. Finally, other dream interpreters will speak of collective symbols, archetypes and the collective unconscious. I am aware of all this. But in itself, their assertions are useful only to pass time or to obtain diplomas. But for a seeker of truth, all these elements are but a waste of time. A seeker of truth, a follower of spirituality, a disciple are all like a sick person: such a person has acknowledged that he is not well and that something essential, the very essence of his being, is missing. But still he rises and goes to find it. There is nothing mysterious about this, but the majority of people do not do it; they let themselves be seduced and end up wasting the little time they have left.

How much money have I spent on therapists and dream interpreters? How many trips have I made to meet them face to face? But essentially all I was looking for was attention, someone who I could tell my dreams to because I have had all kinds of impressive dreams. I followed all the instructions that were given to me, but the deeper I dug into these details about symbols and collective memory, the more confused I became. It's all about the mind's game. Too much detail, too much ambiguity. But the mind likes this – too much so – in order to deviate from its course, and it is in all these details that the mind finds its hiding places, its pretexts, its excuses, its loopholes, and especially its lies.

There is only one tool for understanding dreams, and it is the same tool that is used for understanding life and the whole universe. It is the ultimate and singular tool for understanding oneself. This tool is You. Not you the ego, but You in terms of consciousness – the consciousness at the centre of your being. You just have to get to know it. This consciousness knows everything, and the more you are familiar with your ego, the more you know yourself. And the more you know yourself, the better you will know your fellow human beings, life and its meaning as well as the universe.

There is no need to pay attention to the details, the setting, the collective symbols and even less so the archetypes. Dreams are an assembly of thoughts, and thought is a lie, and therefore waste in a bin. Why rummage around extensively in a bin? What will you find in there? There's no need to rummage – sleep peacefully and pay no attention to anything instead. Sleep exists so that you relax. Your consciousness, which has never slept since the dawn of time, sees what takes place before a dream. In fact, it does not see the dream, it is the dream. Your consciousness manifests in the form of a dream to speak with you. Consciousness speaks to you through a dream for example to show you at most only one or two things, that's all. It does this itself. You have no need to reflect on it. When you wake up, you will instantly know what the dream came to tell you. It's your consciousness that is going to receive the message and deliver it to you when you are awake. Try it out and you will see for yourself. It's not up to you to do anything while you sleep. Just rest and sleep peacefully.

The Real Work In Interpreting Dreams

For its part, the real work does not take place after dreaming as therapists will tell you; nor does it take place during the dream either. It takes place before you dream: in the preceding days. Making the 'witness' grow within you is preparation for this. Vigilance must increase.

It makes no difference whether you are awake or asleep, the more consciousness grows, the more it occupies space in your being. When you sleep, the consciousness that has gained ground during the day wins more of it during sleep. You will see your dreams become clearer, and you will also directly see the connection with the events of the preceding days and this dream without exerting any effort. From the moment that you wake up, you will immediately grasp the relationship between your dream and your experiences of the days leading up to it. I repeat, without any effort. There is no work that you have to do to interpret your dreams other than be vigilant on a daily basis, and you will instantly know of what you have not come to terms with and what you have had bad experiences of, and by consequence, what you have to pay attention to in the future.

The more you practise the quality of bearing witness to things, the better you will be able to see the connections between your dreams and past events, and the clearer your dreams will be. Not in the sense of a film's clarity for example, but you will clearly distinguish between the message of the dream (of any dream for that matter) and the useless details that you can immediately throw in the bin. You will clearly perceive the difference between the essential part of the dream and the information that accompanies it which has no major importance or significance.

And what is the cherry on top of the cake here? It is that in capturing more and more the true sense and the true message of your dreams, you will work on the real problems that you carry around in you. The well-hidden emotional knots deep within your heart. Because your consciousness knows your entire being, it shows you the sites where you have work to do. Is it not a wonderful gift from heaven? And the second cherry on the top of the cake you will receive is that the more you work on yourself by using what dreams show you, the less dreams you will have. Because, quite simply, you will resolve a lot of the emotional knots within you and the amount of dreams you have will gradually reduce until the day comes when you no longer dream more than once a month and then only 3 or 4 times a year.

Here is an example for you: Do you remember the Madelaine McCann case? The little three-year-old English girl who disappeared in 2007 in Portugal. The parents had left the three year old and her two twin sisters who were two years old asleep in their hotel room alone.

That night, whilst the children were sleeping, guess what the parents were doing? They went to dinner with a couple of friends in a tapas restaurant 120 meters from their bungalow. Nine days before their fourth anniversary, Maddie was taken and the bedroom window was left open. I like to watch this type of documentary, I find it interesting. There you have it how my mind has lied to me. In reality, it is because I am afraid that my daughter will disappear or that she will be taken because of lack of focus on my part. And so to avoid this happening, I watch these types of documentaries hoping to learn of new strategies to recognise sex offenders before they take my daughter.

One summer's day, I thought of taking my three year old daughter out to a busy playground. After the idea crossed my mind, I decided against it. That night I had a dream in which I was with my wife and our daughter at a fête and our daughter was walking just in front of us. I was in charge of watching her and I remember worrying in the dream: ‘do not lose sight of her’. There was an enormous amount of people and I ended up losing her for a moment. I immediately found her again and we had a lot of fun in the park.

You see, some years beforehand, this type of dream would easily have been classed as ‘not interesting’ to me. Not only for me, but for the majority of us. The dream is not spectacular, but for a truth-seeker, for those who truly want to progress along the path of self-awareness, the dream is revealing.

This dream revealed to me two truths: The first being the fear that I carried within myself. All the other things in the dream are of no importance. As to knowing whether this fear was of losing or of being responsible for a loss is just a small detail. The important aspect was the fear I felt. My daughter is only the trigger because I already had this fear well before she was born.

The second truth that this dream revealed to me is even more important than the first. It is the fact that I failed the instant this fear took hold of me. This instant is the moment that ‘I thought of taking my three year old daughter out to a busy playground’. On that day, in that moment, just after having had this idea, another thought had crossed my mind. This thought went wrong. In other words, I was not aware of the thought and therefore identified with it without actually realising it. This thought generated my fear, and I have felt the effects of it, but only later on: I was already carried away with this thought and I did not realise it. And that is what is interesting about the dream: making me see that I had handled my emotions 'badly'. Even if sometimes we directly realise something, we can still realise something and handle it badly all the same.

The spiritual ways prepare us for these moments: being present in the moment when an event occurs, when a thought rises to the surface, when we get carried away with our emotions. Be present in yourself in order to perceive and properly experience this moment in harmony with yourself. If these moments pass by without us noticing them, sometimes our consciousness makes us perceive it through a dream. In this way, we will be wiser and more vigilant on the next occasion.

After this dream I had, I became aware of a deep fear that I had been carrying in me for a long time without even knowing it. Now I am more lucid about all that concerns going out with my daughter or going out alone. I am more lucid not to protect my daughter but to recognise the fear the moment it arises and to be able to handle it well.

How to understand the interpretation of dreams according to Sigmund Freud

Dr. Sigmund Freud was a scientist, and scientists study the object and not the subject.

The object, 'from the Latin objectum, etymologically signifies that which is thrown in front of our eyes, or more generally speaking, before our consciousness'. Thus, the object is that which is perceived by the subject, of which the subject becomes aware. The subject is that which perceives, which becomes aware. In our western societies, science only focuses on the object, and scientific studies have gone so far as to break down an object's matter in to its smallest particles, so small that we are not able to split it up any further. The progress of science has been immense in its various domains: to cite but a few, thanks to medicine we nowadays have a much longer life expectancy than in the past, and thanks to technology we can move around more quickly by means of planes and trains and can even go into space. But on the other hand we have forgotten about the subject. In the Orient, particularly in India, much focus is on the study of the subject rather than the object.

In other words, phenomena emerge all the time. The subject is aware of it, and in order to act, has the choice between two essential directions:

The subject can take an interest in the phenomenon as such, or in the phenomenon in relation to itself, the subject. What does this mean in concrete terms? Let us assume that I am a scientist and I have a slug in front of me. I am the subject and the slug is therefore the object. Personally, slugs make me shiver. On the one hand, I have the responsibility of studying the slug in as much detail as possible: the medicine concerning this animal, its anatomy, biology, psychology, the physics that applies to this species, the chemical reactions that take place in it… the list goes on. Western scientists go further in this direction of study, as subjects, as matter: the objects that surround us. On the other hand, I have the possibility of studying not the slug but myself in relation to the slug. In other words, to study the fact that I get shivers when I see a slug for example. Somebody else might not feel anything when looking at this animal and even be capable of touching it. But that disgusts me. Why? Why me? These questions are of the same nature as the larger questions you sometimes ask yourself when phenomena stir more in you than simple shivers at the sight of a slug: 'Why do I suffer?', 'Why is there so much evil on this planet?', 'Why am I on earth?'

… and in this way we enter into a different world, but one that runs parallel to the world of modern science that we know today: It is the world of religion and spirituality.

If physics and chemistry and sciences, religion and spirituality are also sciences in their own right. The former focus their research on the study of matter, of the object perceived by the subject, and the latter on the subject itself. It is not without reason that the spiritual master Sant Rajinder Singh Ji Maharaj calls the spiritual path he teaches the 'Science of Spirituality'.

You may say to me that Western science has also studied the subject through psychology and psychoanalysis for example. No. Your human body is not the subject. Neither is your thoughts, nor your mind, nor your past, nor your future. Neither is your emotions nor your psyche. All these things are a part of the object of which the subject becomes aware. The subject is your consciousness. Even if thoughts manifest in the first person singular or plural such as 'I' am a woman, thoughts are not part of the subject. It is even because of this confusion (among other things) that we believe that the thoughts we have represent us – that they are a voice inside us which guides us.

As physicists and chemists observe and analyse the material, the truth-seekers and the religious believers study themselves in order to know what is hidden in their deepest depths, the very essence of being. And in Asia, particularly India, one finds many more men and women who have managed to discover and experiment with the subtlest forms of consciousness: self-awareness.

In other traditions we call this Enlightenment, self-awakening, Nirvana, Atma, God, Heaven or beatitude. And in order to conduct these studies and investigations on themselves they analysed various things, in particular things such as thoughts, emotions, desires, machinations, actions and reactions, dreams, etc.

In any science, one can consider any object they wish of course, but if the object is not appropriate for that science, the results will differ and be less remarkable. Take the wind for example, it will provide a lesson to a spiritual follower like: 'if a strong wind blows away the roof of my house, it is because it was the will of God!', 'Inshallah!'. But the wind would provide much more to a physicist: he can calculate the speed, force and potency of it… he can convert it into energy and supply an entire city, or use it to make planes fly, or lower parachutes, etc. the list is extensive.

Having said all this, it is clear that a scientist, such as Sigmund Freud who focused his research on an object such as dreams, will surely find results. But these results will be different to those that a spiritual follower would discover when studying the same dream.

Dreams are valuable tools for the study of the Subject, just like the wind is in the field of physics. Dr. Freud is famous for his studies on dreams, but he continued to dream and have nightmares until the end of his life. I, on the other hand, only dream rarely. So allow me to speak to you of dreams and how I freed myself of them.

Dreams are phenomena directly linked to the subject. It's an aide to show you, in its limited form, the things that it missed during the day due to lack of lucidity. From a certain point of view, dreams are a phenomenon that elude science. Science can observe the presence of dreams with the help of modern machines which calculate frequencies the brain emits. Who knows if the machines are already capable of detecting consciousness nowadays. But if they were already capable of it, medical science would not be able to help the consciousness heal from its ills: the mind, all its emotions and all its rules. By improving one or two aspects here and there, yes, it could help; but to heal it completely? No, science is not capable of this. Dreams are one of the tools that the supreme consciousness has made available to help humans know themselves and overcome their problems. Medicine cannot do anything in this area that is beyond it. It is the domain of 'other doctors', those who heal the soul. In some languages, it is even the name given to priests: the doctors of God, 'Nganga Nzambe'.

It is our consciousness that becomes aware of dreams. Science will never know how to go about studying dreams. It belongs to the spiritual domain. Maybe science can one day in the future, but not at present.

In order to interpret dreams, Freud invented four concepts which allowed him to translate the language of dreams into our spoken language:

'Condensation' is when several ideas are amalgamated and become one. Thus, a single element of a dream can conceal several underlying thoughts in a dream.

'Displacement' is to discover the facts that have been inverted in the dream. For example, Mr. Dupont being represented as being poor in your dream although he is a rich man in reality.

'Considerations of representability' is to re-establish the connections that a dream has concealed. For example, two people may be represented in a dream as one person or may be represented by a single thing or aspect that they have in common.

‘Secondary revision’, in which ‘it is a question of ordering the material of a dream in order to make it coherent and intelligible’, according to Catherine Maillard in ‘Le Reve, Histoire et significations’ (2003).

This is all to give meaning to details that contribute nothing to our well-being except to create an entire science, gain university diplomas and even set up a business and earn money from it. There are even those who have created an entire community based on a single detail from a film: Jediism, for example. ‘The order of the Jedi is a fictional organisation created by George Lucas in the cinematographic Star Wars series’. In the films, there is a Jedi philosophy and the Star Wars’ fans have made ‘a new non-theistic and non-organised religious movement based on the philosophical and spiritual teachings of the Jedi. And if this religion can make you smile, it should not be taken lightly because the commitment of the fans has no limit. In England, there is even a school to become a Jedi master. In any case, in some anglophone countries, more than 500,000 people have indicated that their religion is Jedi after the Jedi phenomenon in 2001. Moreover, there are at least three registered and organised Jedi 'temples' (which correspond to churches) in the United States and the United Kingdom'.

J.R.R. Tolkien is a familiar name to you if you have seen the 'Lord of the Rings' trilogy. 'Tolkien was a linguist who was fascinated by languages. He reportedly began creating his fictional Elvish languages around 1910, and his major work in this field is the creation of all the languages spoken throughout Middle Earth. His work in this field is colossal, but the two principal languages that he created are Quenya and Sindarin which are the most well-known because they are the most complete.

So if you are bored or still undecided between German or Spanish, why not choose to learn Tolkien's languages instead? You will most likely never be bilingual in Elvish (you will probably never have an opportunity to use it!) but you will have an entire world to study!', writes Camille Gondral in "Langues inventées: Tolkien et les langues de la Terre du Milieu" (2018).

There is nothing to decipher in dreams unlike Dr. Freud's claims in his work on dreams; there are no symbolism to analyse. Even the most mysterious dream in existence will simply convey either the emotions or rules that your mind cherishes. Dreams just want to convey to you a specific emotion or sentiment. Freud goes to great lengths to make sense of the details in dreams – details that are actually only there to make dreams seem credible and true, at least during sleep. Without these details we would not take dreams seriously and emotions would not arise in us during sleep and finally, we would not think to make the link between dreams and our daily life.

The wise say that everything is an illusion. But this illusion only has power over us because we believe it. How is it that we believe in it? It's because of the details. How is it that we are awe-struck by a good magic trick? Everyone knows that magicians use gadgets to accomplish their tricks, and with the help of these gadgets, they create an illusion and we are fascinated by it.

How is it possible? Because of the details. They make it real, they bring it to life, they are convincing. These details have to be perfect for the illusion to have an effect, just like in magic tricks and in films.

I'm not against the invaluable work Freud has produced on dreams. The famous doctor will remain a pioneer in this field and his studies have left their mark in universities and in hospitals. But it has no place in the heart of our being. It does not advance us in our search for inner peace. I have consulted psychoanalysts and psychologists in order to understand dreams that terrified me at the time. I have also consulted dream interpreters, but none of them have been able to make me see clearly why I was dreaming and how to use their dream interpretations for my well-being despite their qualifications. Their analyses only left me more confused than I was before. If you travel down the same path I was on at the time, you will come to realise that your dreams will not decrease despite these dream interpretations. There are always all kinds of dreams to be had and I promise you it will never end. Freud himself dreamed until the end of his life because he continued to write down his dreams. Psychologists and psychoanalysts also dream.

Doctors are brilliant people. But in the field of dreams, they are the blind leading the blind. Carl Gustav Jung put it well: 'if someone wants to become a psychotherapist, he has to try out the method on himself' ('Wenn jemand Psychotherapeut werden will, dann muss er die Methode am eigenen Leib durchleben'). This is a direct criticism of Freud who had people he did his experiments on instead. All his theories are just pieces of 'knowledge' without having experimented on himself. Just theories to put on paper without any concrete experience. C.G. Jung spoke honestly. I would even say more, it is not only a question of experimenting with the method on oneself, but also to conduct the experiment through to the end and cure the sickness. If not, what is the point of interpreting dreams if not to free oneself of them?

Why seek therapists to understand our dreams? It is because dreams awaken questions within us on our doubts, fears, hopes, etc. We go there in the hope of finding an explanation that would help us to understand ourselves, to suffer less. Yes, to no longer suffer. The simple act of looking for an answer is because we suffer, we are not at peace. We feel an emptiness that we seek to fill. In truth, I tell you, there is no better dream interpreter than the dreamer himself. The only thing he needs to accomplish this task is vigilance. We will come back to this, but first of all we will speak of the different types of dreams.

Types of Dreams

There are innumerable books dealing with the topic of dreams and there are also authors who set out different types of dreams. I am not going to linger on this here, I'm just going to touch on some of these types of dreams. After having read this, you will know where to situate those that I have not addressed in these pages. The examples that I am going to present belong to the most 'mysterious' and appealing kinds of dreams that can raise doubts and questions within us in relation to the interpretation of the dreams that I propose in this book.

Prophetic Dreams

Is the type of dream that warns us of a forthcoming event. Yes, sometimes it occurs, but much more rarely than you might think for that matter. A prophetic dream involves that which was foreseen in the dream being reproduced in real life. Yes, it even flatters one's self esteem as one believes oneself to be amazing and privileged or special for having such an ability, that one is blessed, etc. This is not bad and has its own significance as well.

The premonitory dream's warning is only one aspect of what that same dream is offering us. If we focus on this premonitory aspect of the dream rather than perceiving what valuable revelation the dream provides us with concerning what we have failed to notice in the preceding days, then we are missing the point. These are the clues that help us to see clearly in our daily actions, to see how the mind deceives us, to see the emotions that still reign in us and especially to see what we were unable to when we were awake.

If you let yourself be impressed by the dream's prediction, you are going to dwell on it and lose time and energy. You will continue to live according to your fears, hopes and judgements. The prediction never removed emotions, neither fear nor judgements nor malice. It at least helps you to take measures, but even these measures you take on board under the influence of emotions. And this will continue until you die. Because even if one day you dream that you will die, you will suffer greatly because you will not have been prepared for it. In effect, by privileging the premonitory aspect, you do not prepare yourself and you do not emotionally mature. But life has and always will have hard moments in store for you; even with the best premonitory dreams, you will not escape this suffering. On the other hand, if you focus more on the essential aspect of a dream, you will have a far better understanding of where your weaknesses lie and what it is that you could have observed about the functioning of your mind on the eve of the dream. Thanks to this, you will emotionally mature and you will have a better quality of life even in the most difficult moments.

That's why Christ said 'In this world you will have trouble. But take heart! I have overcome the world' (John 16:33, Bible). Christ is nothing other than the Witness within us, the one who is neither influenced by emotions nor circumstances of life whether they be unpleasant or good. And it is more often through practising lucidity that we gain this quality of the witness.

One of the most well-known dreams of this type is of the Egyptian pharaoh that Joseph had been able to interpret (Genesis 41, Bible). We do not know with certainty whether this event actually took place in this way or if this story is parabolic to make us understand something. But in order to continue, let's accept it as a true story. The pharaoh dreamed of seven healthy cows which were then consumed by seven leaner cows. "Then Pharoah woke up" (Genesis 41:4). That same night he had another dream of the same kind, but this time with seven thin cobs replacing seven fat ones. "In the morning his mind was troubled, so he sent for all the magicians and wise men of the Egypt. Pharaoh told them his dreams, but no one could interpret them for him" (Genesis 41:8). This dream spoke of Egypt's future that was to follow over the course of the next 14 years and how to handle it. It was Joseph, a young Hebrew slave imprisoned in Egypt who made sense of the Pharaoh's dreams. Egypt would then experience seven years of plentiful supply followed by seven years of extreme drought like never before. And the Pharaoh, impressed by the slave, appointed him as the second highest authority in the country after himself, from slave to chancellor of the country along the Nile.

All this is wonderful for Joseph's glory after suffering so much in his life, having been sold by his brothers so as not to kill him, having lived as a slave most of the time and not to mention his time in prison and the false accusations of rape. And the entire country of Egypt would benefit from his help, escaping the misfortunes of famine. It is true that the dignity of Egypt is also the dignity of its sovereign Pharaoh. But what did this dream do for Pharoah himself? What did this dream show him in regard to his own state of mind, his fears, his nightmares?

Firstly this dream was on the one hand a nightmare. The dream woke him up in the night having agitated and terrified him. The fact that it is a nightmare shows that what the Pharaoh experienced a few hours beforehand was an event that had profoundly touched him, even traumatised him, and thus he had not been able to come to terms with it. Had he been more vigilant in the previous days, he would have perceived the link between the dream and the earlier event. And the prophecy of the dream would have been an added bonus.

On the other hand, since the dream is a nightmare, it thereby shows that he has deep fears that have been badly handled and badly digested. Had he been vigilant, he would have realised with certainty what the fears were.

Even the greatest interpreter of dreams would not have been able to help him in this respect, quite simply because he would not have known what the pharaoh had experienced in the few hours before the dream took place. That is why I say that there is no better interpreter of our dreams than ourselves. It concerns the aspect of the dream that is beneficial to our own well-being, for our self-understanding. A dream interpreter could only help in part. Just as Joseph helped save Egypt and save himself. But that part is no more important than the part the pharaoh missed – the part that would reveal his own inner demons to him.

In other words, thanks to Pharaoh's dream, Egypt experienced a period of growth. Joseph was also raised up, but the Pharaoh himself did not develop as a person and remained childish, terrified and tormented by his fears. There would even be a thousand other dreams of this kind, and the Pharaoh would suffer each time. And believe me, if someone were to ask him his opinion, he would say: 'I am fed up with these dreams! … I want to sleep peacefully".

I am going to take this further: his fear was so great that he no longer even had trust in his ministers to the point of abandoning his responsibilities. His ministers had been running the country for a long while and they had done a rather good job of it considering Egypt was still doing well. But the Pharaoh went so far as to humiliate them to such an extent by placing a slave in a position of power above them.

Even if Joseph spoke the truth, do not forget what a slave represented in this period. Moreover, he was a stranger. At worst, he had no more value than a dog. But the pharaoh had raised him to the rank of Prime Minister even though, until his appointment, Joseph's interpretation had not yet been proven true. For this to happen it was necessary to wait seven more years. All of this is to show the extent to which the pharaoh was desperate and terrified by his deepest fears that he was no longer thinking like an adult. He could have appointed Joseph as an advisor and left his ministers to take action for example. What a true lack of trust.

Through fear, he abandoned his responsibilities. By placing Joseph in charge, he did not only bestow him with power, but also that which goes with it, like a twin sister: the weight of responsibility. All he had to do was watch him. His ministers as well. If Joseph made an error, it would be easier to cut off his head rather than one of his ministers, a son of the country. The dream would have been able to show him all this, because all his fears and this lack of confidence was within him even before the dream came about. The dream no doubt just triggered them. As an individual, the pharaoh missed good opportunities that were offered to him on a golden plate by the dream.

There are so many books on premonitory dreams. Don't let yourself be seduced by these fabulous tales. Concentrate on the aspect of the dream that is going to heal you. And when you are healed, the twists and turns in life matter little, you will lead a good life, in peace and well-grounded in yourself. Learn to catch fish yourself rather than be content to receive one. Even if the premonitory dream could save your grandmother from death, help her of course, but never forget the aspect of the dream that reveals your thoughts and fears to you. Because this will heal you and the prophecy will also save your grandmother. But if you save your grandmother and forget the other aspect of the dream then you will suffer, perhaps for the rest of your life.

Lucid Dreams

This is the type of dream in which one is aware of the fact that one is dreaming. In these dreams, the dreamers are "capable of reason, remember their waking life and can act freely – either reflectively or according to courses of action established before sleep. Nevertheless they remain deeply asleep, living in a vivid dream world that seems astonishingly real", according to Stephen LaBerge (L'art de diriger ses rêves). But it is necessary to add that during a lucid dream, the controlled part is considerably smaller than the rest of the dream that continues along its course just like in any other dream. It is 10 to 20% of dreams, maybe even less, that are controlled. In this type of dream the controlled aspects are often the decisions and choices that can consciously be made. It is not that someone chooses the dream's theme, the setting or the people. I am speaking from my own experience and of the experiences of those with whom I have done my work with on dreams.

At one time someone told me that they went to see African marabouts in order to do me harm. The idea of someone going to consult the marabouts to cause me harm had terrified me over the following weeks and I had the same dream several times. In this dream, two creatures came to apprehend me and take me with them. The first forcefully grabbed me by my right arm and the second by my left. They were so strong that I was not able to free myself from their grip no matter how much I struggled. They made fun of me whilst at the same time telling me that it was over for me, that it was the end. They flew away with me laughing and together we entered the depths of the darkness before us. I refused, I struggled without success. In my opinion it was the sorcerers who wished me harm. As I had been raised in an African Christian family who visited prayer groups, in order to drive the two creatures away, I began to pray: 'in the name of Jesus Christ, I cast you out. Be gone!" I prayed harder and harder, as though the name of Jesus was more effective if I said it louder! I woke up with a start shouting "in the name of Jesus!". I had this dream more than three times, and each time was exactly the same until I conquered this fear in my waking state: the fear of being devoured by demons.

The correct interpretation of this dream was that I had a strong fear of being the victim of a spell. And this fear had reached its peak when a friend of mine had been found dead in his bedroom. According to rumours, he was the victim of a magic spell. I was traumatised by the fear of ending up like him, dying so young, murdered by jealous people. In the African society I grew up in, almost everyone believes in witchcraft. Especially in Central and West Africa, witchcraft occupies a very large place in the traditions. I grew up with this fear. After having overcome this fear in my daily life, I was ready to confront the two evils in my dream. I knew what I was going to do if they came back : give in. Wherever they wanted to take me, I would no longer resist. Evidently I had the same dream again on another occasion and that time was the last. There I was, waiting for them to come. When they came back, they did what they have done before: grab me one on each side and take me with them. In accordance with my plan, I swore to myself to go to the end with them this time, to go see what was in the darkness, and if it meant never coming back, then so be it. I did not struggle, I did not try to cast out these demons in the "name of Jesus". They flew away with me in peace, entered the darkness and the dream finished just like that, without me abruptly waking up. I woke up calmly in the morning. And from that day on, I have been free from these beliefs in witchcraft, of spells that can be cast on me to destroy my life, etc.

This series of dreams is also mysterious. In order to interpret them, I would have to spend time analysing elements such as: the unconscious, the collective unconscious, symbols and archetypes, I would never have been able to free myself from this fear. I consulted therapists and dream interpreters about it. They provided me nothing apart from knowledge and a wider vocabulary in this field. Speaking of vocabulary, I have just discovered that there are even dream dictionaries. In these dictionaries can be found dream symbols that are supposed to help people identify hidden messages behind each image or message seen in their dreams. It's great for business: dictionaries can be sold. For those who just want to tell themselves and others about the wonderful stories they have had in their sleep, these dictionaries and symbols are amazing. If you have the time, please do. But for the truth-seeker, the true disciple who truly wants to heal the mind and discover inner peace, then to go searching for the hidden meaning in objects and messages in dreams is a senseless undertaking, a waste of time.

As for lucid dreams, some claim they are able to go further and be capable of controlling their dreams. Not just being aware that they are dreaming, but also truly being able to control and manipulate the course of the dream.

Who knows if they are telling the truth. Personally, I do not believe it if I have not experienced it myself. A true disciple is not content with rumours. They go and verify it. I therefore started practising this art, but I quickly became disinterested. As soon as I understood the real interpretation of dreams, I knew what to expect. Rather than venturing into the world of dreams, I preferred to be satisfied with taking dreams as they came, examining them through vigilance in my daily life, healing from them so as not to dream anymore. But there are enough techniques for learning to dream consciously. Everyone is free to practise them or not as they choose.

There are even specialists who present lucid dreaming as a therapy for combatting nightmares or phobias by intervening in the course of the dream or by preventing them all together. For what purpose? Dreams, even the most banal, are themselves the ultimate therapy. Unless you are mad or crazy in believing that you are smarter than the self-awareness within you to change the course of dreams. And if you succeed in doing so and you manage to change the course of your dreams, then you are distorting the game. Your dream will certainly be interesting in accordance with your fantasies, but you will have destroyed the message that the dream was bringing to you in order to perceive your mind at work and to know yourself.

To be able to control your dreams is a very attractive idea. It is also a distraction. The mind likes this kind of thing and will convince you that it is important and that it can help you. It is the Devil's lie. The Devil is nothing other than our mind. That is the evil one the Bible speaks of. The mind is the liar. It is not our ally, it is our adversary – the adversary of the ego and self-awareness. It certainly is a tool for our consciousness, but this tool is broken, dysfunctional. If the mind wins, you lose.

Dreams naturally show you the functioning of the mind that you have not been able to see through lack of vigilance. Why then try to change the course of a dream? You will have missed a good opportunity to get to know yourself deeply and grow, winning more and more peace of mind. Fortunately, there is the possibility of developing lucidity, vigilance, self-presence. This is what we are going to see now.

LUCIDITY

The Witness

Some people remember their dreams when they wake up whereas others rarely remember them. According to Perrine Ruby, a researcher of cognitive neuroscience, in order to remember a dream our brain needs to encode it in our long-term memory. When you are asleep, the brain is not capable of carrying out this procedure. Therefore, it must wake up briefly in order to encode the dream in our long-term memory so as to be capable of relating it back to us when we wake up. According to research, it has also been demonstrated that those who dream a lot – the 'big dreamers' - wake up briefly more often than the 'small dreamers'.

We may not remember our dreams every time, but we always know that we have dreamed. It is for this reason that we often find ourselves saying 'I do not remember my dream'. Who has never said this before? We admit to knowing that we dreamed at some point in the night when we say this, even if the content of the dream eludes us. Due to the fact that our consciousness never sleeps, we always know that we have dreamed. The dream takes place within our consciousness, the brain also operates within our consciousness, as is memory found within the heart of our consciousness.

Consciousness keeps watch over all this. Even if we do not remember our dream, the information of the dream is still there, engraved in our memory. It is just that the link between the neurons is no longer established.

If we dream but do not remember it, it is because we are divided amongst our thoughts in our daily lives – we have been distracted, carried away by fortunate or unfortunate events alike, carried away by our emotions and thoughts. We are exposed to so many impressions and so much information throughout the day that we absorb without realising. I am not talking about concentration (or a lack thereof), I speak of self-presence. One can be focused without being present in oneself. It is possible to concentrate for several minutes on something whilst at the same time not being vigilant.

The position of the witness is key, not only to interpreting all dreams, but also to happiness. The witness, called 'Sakshi' in Sanskrit, has a special characteristic: neutrality. It is the spectator. It neither judges nor passes comments. Like a witness to a crime, it sees what happens, and that is all.

By means of this neutrality, the Witness is the only part within us that is able to detach itself from the mind. It is not a part of the mind's game in which the mind is the expert in judgement. You can adopt the position of the inner witness, being a spectator watching what is happening inside and outside of yourself at any moment wherever you may be. Not ‘you’ as in Ego, but ‘you’ the absolutely neutral Witness who observes the spectacle of other conditioned and determined forms of consciousness: your states of mind, thoughts, emotions, moods, fears, desires, happy states, sad states, …

It is because of this that you are able to be the witness, observer or spectator. Every manifestation of the mind is a part of the spectacle and appears within the field of consciousness, including the dream. The physical body is also a part of it along with everything that is related to it: injuries, sicknesses, birth, death… Every aspect of reality that surrounds us, every aspect in which we are immersed into, is a part of this spectacle. And the witness can observe this without so much as getting involved.

The term ‘witness’ is only a word. In reality, the ‘Witness’ is also another limited form of consciousness, but this limited form is special and unique. It is neutral and represents the bridge between the sense of self and supreme consciousness. We have immediate access to this particular form of consciousness that is the Witness, we only have to help it grow. However, the supreme consciousness eludes us most of the time. This is why it is easier to go through the witness to reach consciousness. By practising assuming the role of the spectator, the more the Witness will grow and the closer we will get closer to supreme consciousness. In other words, the Witness is the seed and ultimate consciousness is the tree, the mature form of the seed. The seed already has the potential to become a tree, it just has to grow to transform from one form to the other.

Take for example your internal conflicts. You are immediately able to bear witness to them as you have access to this capacity at any moment and under any circumstance. Instead of identifying yourself with two poles of the conflict such as: 'I ought not to … but I can't help it', or '…it's wrong… but I can't stop myself', or '…this is the third time that I've decided to stop and yet I'm doing it again..!', you can instead act as the Witness to the conflict rather than letting yourself be torn between two points that lead you in circles. Just observe these poles and let them be, without judging and without commenting. Just observe them. But do not forget: here and now, with or without conflict, I am able to assume the position of the conscious witness. The quality of acting as the witness is always there at your disposal. The nature of the Buddha, Nirvana, the kingdom of heaven, the atman, it's all there. You may not be able to remain in this state of being the witness, but you can access it at any moment and come back as often as you like.

This quality of the Witness has always been there and will remain, it is just veiled by the functioning of the mind which takes up all the space. I mentioned earlier that the term 'Witness' is nothing other than a word for a limited form of consciousness but that this limited form is more accessible to us than consciousness itself. As a means of understanding this, take the example of clouds overlaying the sun: you cannot directly see the sun, but you know it is there behind the clouds no matter how large they are. The clouds are in front of you, not the sun. The clouds are comparable to the mind – we can reach forth and clear them away in order to see the sun again. And in order to pierce the clouds, we only need to adopt the position of the witness.

Whatever your emotional situation or state of mind is, be it depression, shame, happiness, sadness, etc., the position of the witness is always available to you. Perhaps you will not reach nirvana straight away, but you will benefit from a detachment from your mind and your environment. But we as humans ignore it most of the time and identify ourselves with various limited forms of consciousness which are contradictory and painful.

The most effective way of explaining this is by using cinema or theatre as an example. Let's imagine that Leonardo DiCaprio has to play the role of Romeo in the film 'Romeo and Juliet'. The director is Supreme Consciousness, God, Allah, or however else you want to call him. Romeo (or Juliet for women), is you, me, every human being, and the film is our life here on earth, the spectacle, our entire universe, Shiva's dance. The actor Leonardo DiCaprio (who we shall call Leo henceforth for conciseness) is the Witness. He is inserted into the role of Romeo, but Leo never once forgot throughout filming that he is not actually Romeo. If he begins to confuse the character he is playing with himself, Leo will end up in a psychiatric ward. He plays Romeo knowing all the while that Romeo is not part of him and that he will not actually die after the poison scene with Juliet.

Leo knows that Juliet does not love him, but Romeo, who he is playing. All the problems that arise in the film, all the emotions Romeo experiences for Juliet, are just a part of this spectacle just as is the relationship between the two lovers also. Leo just plays his part and is content to spectate without passing judgement. It's none of his business to anyway. Whether the film ends badly or not is not a problem for him. And it is this position of the witness that spirituality proposes that we take up because the Witness deep within us is outside of the problems of daily life.

I am not speaking about improving one or more aspects of our lives, that is not what the Witness is concerned with. Such things do not bother the witness because in reality these things are not really a problem. The problems of Romeo are not a problem for Leo. He will be happy to play that which the script dictates to him. After all, it is already written, there is nothing to change. If Leo begins to try to improve Romeo's problems, then believe me he will be turned away from the project and at worst he will end up in psychiatric treatment. All he has to do is play his part well. To change or improve Romeo's problems is not a worry of the witness.

Improving an aspect, or perhaps several aspects, of your life is what psychologists and other similar professionals offer us help with. On the contrary, spirituality invites us to detach ourselves completely from it all, to go beyond our normal way of life and the problems we face every day that prevent us from living in peace despite the tribulations of life.

Medicine offers us the possibility of healing the physical body, whilst spirituality offers us total freedom from the physical body whether it be suffering from a sickness or not. Psychology offers us the possibility of healing or changing subtle things (less timidity, less aggression, less violence, more self-confidence, detachment from harmful thoughts and painful memories, ...), whilst spirituality offers us complete freedom from these subtleties and all those psychological and psychic mechanisms.

Those who have already approached a Sage know what I am talking about: how these people, these Sages, are free from their physical bodies even if they are carrying some illness. A well-known example comes from Dr. Roger Godel's book 'Essais sur l'expérience libératrice' in which he speaks about his trip to India to meet Ramana Maharshi who was suffering from cancer in his shoulder. As a doctor, Godel had not seen someone before whose body was in such awful condition yet still shined so brightly with such a pure look. In general, those who are healthy pity the sick, but in the case of Ramana Maharshi it was the sick who felt sorry for themselves, feeling so small before a man sick with cancer. Ramana Maharshi was beaming with joy despite his rotting cancerous shoulder.

Being the witness does not mean doing nothing. By observing your inner conflict without judging, you will understand what you must do if it is possible to improve your situation. The main thing is not your actions but the position of the witness. Action will be automatic and pure if it comes from the Witness and not the Ego. This is always accessible, whatever your external or internal situation is. There are never any exceptions. The mind is very skilled at making you believe that there are exceptions and that when emotions are very painful there is no way for you to be the witness. This is false. It is also why the Bible calls the mind the 'the devil'. There is never an exception. You are always able to be witness to some situation and to respond to it if necessary. To forget this possibility of the Witness is the only sin that is unforgiveable. (Matthew 12:30-31, Bible). 'Sin' signifies 'error' (I am not the one asserting this, it is justifiable, but it will be a topic to cover another time.). Error in relation to what? Error in relation to happiness. If you forget to be the Witness to a spectacle then you are responsible for your failed happiness. And what is your own fault is never forgivable. But there is good news: it is never too late.

When you find yourself in a difficult situation, come back to yourself and ask the question: 'am I perfectly happy?'. 'no'. 'but I can be witness to the spectacle' without passing judgement on it. The witness itself is happy beyond the mechanisms of the mind, i.e.: thoughts and emotions.

WHAT GOOD IS LUCIDITY?

This notion of the Witness is what spirituality and religion provide us with. The position of the witness is the way out for all the problems in our lives. The religions and the spiritual paths are there to remind us repeatedly that there is an exit available to us right now and not 'when the suffering has subsided', or 'when I get out of this bad patch'. I am able to be the spectator right here and now and see what happens inside and outside of myself. When you begin to act as the witness everything begins to change, you start to be more conscious of your daily life. As you become more alert to things happening in your life and you no longer identify so much with your mind, you will no longer get carried away with positive or negative emotions for hours on end. It will automatically become easy for you to make the link between a dream and your experiences in the preceding days. It is even easier than that because the connection is self-made. You will know if you dreamed or not when you wake up. If you have dreamed, the link is established by itself. You will simply realise that the dream is directly related to this or that event, and at the same time you will know why you had this particular dream and what you should take from it. Most of the time it is emotions or laws of the mind, which have been formulated since childhood.

In the beginning, this Witness, this vigilance or self-awareness is still very small, but it grows by means of exercise and putting teachings into practise. Every little sprout will take up more and more space in the centre as it grows until it reaches its final form: unlimited consciousness, Nirvana, the kingdom of heaven. This small and insignificant witness in your life today will one day become an integral part in your life whilst the rest will become insignificant.

To summarise: be witness to your life and there is nothing you will not gain from it. Have only the attitude of being a spectator. Arnaud Desjardins always used the example of the vertical dimension in his four volumes entitled 'À la recherche du Soi': Imagine yourself in your car in the middle of a traffic jam unable to move forward for hours. On the radio it is announced that your car has an option that you did not know about until now: it has hidden propellers attached to the roof, you just have to press a button. The emotional or physical difficulties as well as the thoughts that are at the origin of all our problems, are all situated within this horizontal dimension. That is to say in front of, behind, to the left and right of you. As long as you do not know that your 'car' can take on another dimension you will remain stuck where you are as long as the traffic is blocked. But by listening to this news, of course everyone will do the same as you: everyone will press a button and go vertically up to where you are free from traffic and where the road opens up before you. But while you are climbing, the traffic jam is still dense below but it is no longer a problem for you because you have entered into another dimension.

It is the same for the quality of the witness: when you take it on, the ups and downs of your life do not disappear, not straight away at least, but they lose their power over you since the witness is situated on another plane of consciousness that is not within the spectacle.

SOME EXERCISES

The Position Of The Witness

When we get carried away by a strong emotion, this exercise is to acknowledge that we are getting carried away with feeling this emotion and to come back to oneself in order to behold the feeling without judging.

Am I completely happy? No. I'm getting carried away with an emotion. I can realise this and I come back to myself: the attention is then focused on me. I let the emotion run its course. I do not judge it, for the emotion is neither good nor bad. No thoughts like 'it should not be there', 'this is not the right time', 'will it always be me!?', or 'I'm fed up of this!'. Just 'Yes, the emotion is there'. I then focus my attention on something other than my thoughts or emotions. I look for a point of support and then I stick to it.

The point of support can be to let myself feel the emotion, for example the pain I feel from that emotion. The human body, the corporeal, can also be the point of support: my breathing, the feeling of one of my limbs, etc. The third point of support is just to do nothing at all: to empty your mind and reject all thoughts that arise.

As for the first point of support I mentioned above about feeling the pain of an emotion, it is a matter of taking the emotion for what it is, a form of energy, and nothing else. Just as electricity flowing through your body is a form of energy. Thus you should simply feel the emotion and appreciate it while you can without judging or commenting on it, just simply letting it be. In this way, that particular form of energy on a given day will be used up once and for all and will not return to the place it came from.

When there is no emotion present, the exercise is to be aware of yourself and acknowledge what you are in the middle of doing, observing it without judging. The point of reference in this case can be the human body in regard to sensing or acknowledging a body part, or you can simply observe your thoughts without commenting on them or judging them. Simply by observing your thoughts you no longer identify yourself with them and you become witness to them. You could also chase away any thought as soon as it arises without giving it time to express itself.

'ah, this is what I am doing' – I acknowledge it and I come back to myself: the attention is focused on me or a body part. I leave the emotions or thoughts to run their course. I neither judge nor interfere. As I have just mentioned, the point of support for the body can be the breath, a body part or the entire body.

Whatever your chosen point of reference is, you should sense or acknowledge it and appreciate it while you can. For example, make sure to feel the movement and the impact every time your foot hits the ground, the feeling of holding something in your hand, the taste or flavour of what you're eating or even the pain of a wound that is still bleeding or is infected. Pain is also an energy. Sense the energy and how it flows around your body.

Thoughts are going to interrupt you, arise in you, every second; and each time this happens you should start the exercise again from the beginning. It is not a question of thinking about or controlling the body's movements, let the body continue its routine. With practise you will realise this: although the body follows its own procedures, there is another space in which you can place your consciousness without it disturbing the rest of your body's routines. For example you can burst out laughing whilst at the same time being entirely aware that you are in the middle of laughing and that you look like your mother when doing so. In the middle of a conversation as well I can come back to myself and realise that I sound like my father when I speak. I acknowledge that I sound like my father instead of thinking 'oh no, I do not like the way I speak'. Has this kind of realisation ever happened to you before? I believe it has. Even without practise consciousness becomes vigilant. But only sometimes. With practise though, vigilance increases much faster than if one was to let things unfold naturally.

If you plant a seed and let it grow naturally on its own, it is less likely that it will grow to become a tree one day. There are simply too many obstacles for a seed to overcome alone: the seasons which may be favourable or unfavourable towards the growth of the seed, bad weather, drought, or animals that could eat it before the seed has even experienced moist soil. But if you look after the seed and protect it from heavy rain that would flood it, from predators and dryness, etc., then the small seed has a greater chance of reaching maturity and producing amazing fruits. The same goes for lucidity.

It is not necessary to think about or control bodily movements. Do not act like the centipede which begins to control its legs in order to improve its mobility and ends up confusing itself with its legs all entangled. In the end the centipede can no longer walk. Thus it is not necessary to be controlling, but to be present when something occurs, just being witness to it.

This exercise can be done any time without exception. In joy or in sorrow, in pleasure or in suffering, in sport or in intimate moments, when waking up or going to sleep. To forget this is the unforgivable sin because this opportunity is always available to you. If you do not practise this then you have only to blame yourself.

Rather than getting lost in your thoughts (and since you gain nothing from this), enjoy the movements of your body instead.

Rather than getting lost in your emotions, savour the sensation of an emotion, embrace it entirely without judging it. You will see the emotion follow its natural course, increasing in intensity until it reaches its peak then to come down and disappear for good. This energy that you have just experienced in its entirety will never come back again in that way. But if instead you experience an emotion and let yourself get carried away with it, identifying with it and judging it, then it will manifest itself and also reach its highest peak; only that when it disappears, it will not be for good. This is because this energy current will not have been used up entirely, and thus it will go back to where it came from, to its source, the emotional knot or the ball of energy that feeds this particular emotion that you have just let escape. The subject of emotions is a subject to deal with separately. For now, the main point to grasp is that emotion is a form of energy that has its own mechanism, and if you experience it in a certain way it will never return – its source, the emotional knot, loses an ounce of its energy. With time it will shrink until it dies out completely one day. But if you experience it in an inappropriate way, it will not go away after a while, but it will instead go back to feed its source, and it will always return to you until the end of your life.

This exercise allows you to focus your attention not on the problem at hand that has triggered an emotion but on the emotion itself. With this exercise you can leave the mind's game with its thoughts and worries behind. You return to the vertical dimension where there is no worry, just peace, and consciousness will subsequently grow and take up more space in your life.

This is a valuable exercise. You will never be bored again. Boredom consists of going round in circles with your thoughts. By means of this exercise you are no longer a part of the world of thoughts. Instead of reading a magazine in a doctor's waiting room you can do this exercise and spend your time with yourself being witness.

Seated Meditations.

This is the same exercise as the one above except here you are seated. There are various schools that teach different postures, but the most well-known one is the Buddhist Zazen. This form of meditation is all about your posture. Nothing about it is left to chance, however you must respect the attitude and the form that has been strictly taught by the masters who have all practised it: to be sat with your legs crossed, knees against the ground with a straight back, hands out in front between the thighs with the left hand on top of the right with both thumbs touching and without moving. Whatever happens, do not move a muscle, be that to chase a fly away or even to slump. Have your eyes slightly open, and from this stillness of the body all the internal whirlwinds will rise up and face us.

From there it is necessary to adopt the position of the witness, Sakshi, observing everything without judging or moving, not even to adjust your posture. At the same time you will all the internal storms that arise one after another.

This is an exercise that you can do according to your capabilities starting with a few minutes a day. With a bit of practise you will learn how to spend a lot of time like this.

There are also many other postures that exist and by doing some research you will find some that suit you. I personally prefer the first exercise – the position of the witness – that I can do whilst I carry out my daily activities. It can even be practised whilst sitting or laying down. Zazen cannot be, and you must also reserve a part of your day to perform this exercise. But in regard to the position of the witness, there is no specific time set aside to do it, as it is applicable at any time under any circumstance – whilst walking, sitting, lying, anything.

'Tapas'

'Tapas', which in English means asceticism, has always been practised in the spiritual domain as it is a means of accelerating the process to self-realisation. The idea behind Tapas is that Life constantly puts trials in front of us with the goal not of punishing us but making us grow and evolve.

Tapas is a test that a spiritual follower creates for himself in the form of an exercise, a difficulty he puts in front of himself so that he can confront it, practise the exercise and evolve. The Egyptians have used this technique since the time of the pharaohs.

In India, Tapas is well-known. Even Christians use it when fasting for example. The famous discipline in Islam is nothing other than Tapas . According to Islam, the secret to success is discipline: in Ramadan there are the five daily prayers and fasting to name but two things. This Tapas exercise is very effective when done correctly. It is like a stepping stone – a lift that you can use to quickly get to the upper floors without using the stairs. This must be done however in accordance with certain principles. Cheating has no place here. So what is Tapas all about?

It is a matter of surpassing oneself through effort exerted. Is it similar to going outside of your comfort zone? Yes, but mainly with regard to the attitude one should adopt when doing so. Tapas must affect you. The more it shakes you, the more you will progress. Here is a nice example that illustrates clearly what austerity is:

When I was a teenager my family experienced some difficult years. The government suspended the salaries of civil servants for more than six months sometimes, yet my father worked every day. As there were many of us in the house, he could not take care of all of us: school fees were beyond his means, most notably because of the daily travel expenses to go to and return from five schools and three universities, and that is without mentioning food, school uniforms and all the necessary supplies needed that enable you best to learn at school. He decided to send the youngest of us, which was one of my brothers and I, to boarding school as a solution.

At least there were fewer fees to pay there. Thus my brother and I spent a year at boarding school. Practically in the sticks, life was very difficult there, and we returned to our home town during the summer holidays. When it was time to return to the boarding school in the middle of nowhere after the summer holidays, my brother let out a cry from the heart, one that he had been trying to suppress for months: 'NO! I can't take it anymore, I don't want to go back there'. He tried to explain to me that we suffered for no reason at the boarding school where we were deprived of all the benefits available in town such as electricity, drinking water, friends and so on. I did not know what to think. We went to see our parents to whom my brother explained our entire situation and asked them to take us out of the school. I still remember clearly how moved our father was and the look he gave my brother. He looked at me next and asked me the question: 'what are your thoughts on this?'

This question left a deep impression on me. You must know that I am the youngest in my family and they always took care not to leave me alone too far away, like at a school for example. Wherever I went

I always had a 'big brother' who took care of me or at least to whom I could confide in. In brief, I felt I did not receive all the credit for something I accomplished but that whoever was there with me at the time also received a part of the praise. I was thirteen at the time, and, truth be told, until that point no one had ever asked me for my opinion on a subject before.

Thus it was to my astonishment when I heard my father's question. And for my part, what did I think of it? I saw in this question the opportunity to assert myself, to prove to myself that I could very well manage over there so far away from my father, mother, brothers, sisters, friends and all the small luxuries of daily life of which one is deprived of at the boarding school. Through this question I saw the opportunity to grow, to learn, to understand life, far from any protection or guardian. I looked at our father and I responded: 'I will go back and take up the challenge'. And so I went back to the boarding school, not just for one year but for three years running. I went back there with joy and crushed and overcame all the difficulties with pride. Even when it became quite difficult – for it was difficult there; the lack of hygiene was such that we went into the bush just behind the dormitory to relieve ourselves as the toilets were so dirty. It was also necessary to go everyday to the spring to draw water, and let us not even talk about this spring in question.

We can skip over the typhoid fevers and malaria that I frequently used to catch. But I knew deep within myself that if I overcame these tests I would grow. And it is true, the boarding school for me is the time in my childhood that I loved the most because those moments made me a confident young man who had the confidence to go anywhere on earth alone and get by with ease, overcoming all kinds of hardships. Even if I have had many failures, it is the feeling I have within myself that counts.

In this example, I took a difficult situation that life had given me and transformed it into an exercise: Tapas. But there are also situations that you can create for yourself from scratch according to your taste. I once cut off the apartment's heating for a month in the middle of winter when I was a student although I cannot stand the cold. How unpleasant it was to sleep wearing a coat, but I embraced this difficulty joyfully.

For austerity to take effect, your attitude is vital. The exercise will not yield its benefits if you complain or grumble. You will only receive your own discontentment, grumblings and complaints. When it becomes particularly difficult you might begin to cry or be exasperated. This is a natural bodily reaction, but your internal position should not be defensive nor take on the role of the victim.

There is no place for people who view themselves as victims in heaven. It is not because you cry or complain that allows you to have your way. Before a court judge this may work, but this strategy does not work for self-awareness. Be quiet, sit yourself down, roll up your sleeves and fight. Your attitude should be that of a competitor rather – embrace the difficulty and give it your best shot. Stop the exercise early if you are going to take on too much and end up complaining and finish it another time.

When I was a young adult during my student years before my baccalaureate I lived in a state of constant precarity. I did not even have enough money to get myself a cake for my birthday. I would wake up in the morning on my birthday and say 'happy birthday, Cadet' to myself. I wrote this phrase in my diary and drew a cake next to it. I am not the only person to have done this, I have met other people who have done the same thing. But your attitude changes everything. I persevered with great joy without feeling like a victim or feeling abandoned by my own people or forgotten by anyone. After a while, if you maintain a positive attitude very well, you become free and detached from it all. You stay indifferent – whether others think about you or not or remember your birthday or not – sooner or later it no longer matters. But look around you and you will see how much people value birthday parties. Even at eighty years old there are still some people who are offended because someone forgot their birthday. Many will reluctantly tell you 'it's not important' if you forgot their birthday, but deep down they are offended.

If you do this exercise properly, Tapas will present you with its treasure, that is a guarantee.

First of all vigilance will increase because by taking the right attitude towards Tapas one automatically returns to oneself, to the feeling of oneself, that lies deep within us. Self-confidence is something many of us lack, but it will naturally gain ground through these exercises and you will begin to truly believe in yourself and think highly of yourself. Not that self-confidence that can be acquired through conventions in which motivational speakers are good at making you believe that you are amazing and that you just have to believe in certain methods to have confidence in yourself. Sometimes this works for one or two things but at the slightest difficulty you fall back into your doubts. This exercise I speak of here does not concern a third party, as you yourself will experiment with it. You will reexperience a sense of greatness that you have been carrying within you from birth but have lost over the years as a result of the experiences you have had since your childhood: The feeling that nothing in the universe is greater than you. For the universe is already within you, there is no need to go looking outside of yourself. This conviction will grow inside you the more you practise this exercise.

In addition to this, you will also gain the sense that you are self-sufficient. You will depend much less on compliments others give you. What does this signify? 'I know who I am. What I say about myself is more valuable than what the entire country could say about me'.

I am not talking about telling yourself that you are self-sufficient or repeating this phrase in your head, because this means that we again join up with 'motivational speakers'. I have myself also benefitted from this type of discourse, but my doubts came back to me again and again. It is not a question of thinking but of experiencing – living and discovering for yourself like any other type of experience, and no one will ever be able to convince you otherwise nor will any circumstance. You will be on the same wavelength as the motivational speakers that you admire on Youtube or on the television. By practising these exercises you will one day be on their level rather than paying to go listen to their tales. You yourself will have stories to tell when you have done Tapas.

Being a child, everything you did not receive from the people you considered most dear to you in the world (like your parents) along with all the bad things you also received from them will take away a part of your self-confidence each time. A young eight-year-old child who has not done well at school and to whom the father says: 'shame, you are not as intelligent as I was. At your age, I had a mark of 98% in my report'. How do you expect this child to believe in himself afterwards? Throughout his life there is a good chance he will believe that he is not smart even though all he did was spend too much time that year playing and had received 55% in his report as a result. It is not a brilliant mark but he did not fail. But to say such a thing to a child could be disastrous and destroy the child's self-esteem.

Thus we can see people seeking to be admired by others throughout their lives, wanting to receive compliments, be asked to meet up, be regarded, be liked... The compliments that we so often wanted to receive from the people we cherished the most we end up looking for later on in others, the substitutes for our parents in adult life. These small words that we really wanted to hear coming from them: 'well done!', 'yes it is already very good as it is', 'wow, wonderful! We could just change this bit...', 'your drawing is beautiful' even if it is awful. Yes, even if the drawing is awful! It is not up to the parents to beat their children with a stick so to speak, life itself with take care of this anyway. It is up to the parents to build strong feelings in their children through compliments and loving words to name but two things. Yes parents have to educate their children and sometimes be strict with them. But in the beginning it is better to be soft and become stricter with time.

And Tapas reinforces the sense of self, and the more you practise the more this feeling will grow. For every child it is the parents who are the most cherished people. But there is no one greater than you in the universe. Thus, by practising these exercises and outdoing yourself time and time again, one difficulty after another, you gain the sense of self-sufficiency. Even the substitutes you make for your parents will not hold any power greater than that which you know or say about yourself.

Your intuition will have grown, you will know deep down that you are right and no doubt will arise in you even if the whole world is against you. I hope you can experience this one day.

You will begin to provide yourself all that you have been deprived of from compliments to great gifts and from the love you have for yourself to the confidence you have in yourself. What you give yourself has far greater value than that which someone else can offer you. It is a law of nature. You just have to have the right attitude. After all, if you are not able to achieve this for yourself then who can do it for you? Other people are also concerned with their own problems whilst you are there looking out for how they look at you, searching for their opinion on you. Yet the king or queen in your life is yourself. And so I repeat, if you are not able to do anything for yourself, then no one will do it for you. No one will do it better than you anyway. The world could give you all the compliments you wanted to hear, all the love you desired, and even then you could end up killing yourself. There are as many examples of celebrities taking their own lives as there are stars in the sky. Why? Because it is you and you alone who holds the power that you seek in others.

Tapas is first and foremost the attitude of accepting new challenges, of being a good player, the type of person who does not complain when he lets in a goal or receives a knocks. It is to push a little further beyond than the point we have already reached.

'I have set myself thirty days to survive in the cold without heating in my apartment. I'm at twenty-five and I cannot take it any longer. I have a cold and a cough. I cannot do any more of this'. 'But can I hold out until midday? It's currently nine o'clock, let's see'. You hold out until midday and then you start again, managing to get to eight o'clock in the evening the same day. 'it is still too hard. I really cannot go any further. It is over!'. Yes, it is hard, but there is an idea that crosses through your mind: what if I try to get through the night? After all, I am less aware of the cold than when I am awake. Thus you surpass yourself one more time. When it becomes more difficult you count the hours rather than the days. This is what must be done to reach the goal. Next you push yourself to the point where you count the minutes instead of the hours because you cannot take it anymore. At this point it is important to have set some kind of limit by which you move forward and can choose to stop the experiment.

In this example, if you get through the night you will have lived through one more day beyond your strength. Then you reach the morning and the twenty-sixth day has dawned. You think to yourself that you will stop here, but after breakfast you see that deep down you actually had more resources in you than you thought you had. This is the conflict between the laws your mind has made up for itself and the reality in front of you. This is spirituality – not what you think, not dogmas in which you have to believe in, but experience, that which you have lived through. Act and you will see.

EPILOGUE

We all seek perfect happiness, but who is stopping us from achieving this? Have you ever asked yourself this question? Who actually stops you from being happy? Certainly not other people, for if happiness depended on others we would have no chance of finding it, of being at peace. Other people are independent of you; you have no control over them. If someone else holds the key to your happiness it would be difficult to pursue happiness and the spiritual teachings would fall apart. The word 'Other' signifies everything that is not you: other human beings, material objects, even events and circumstances.

It is not other people that take away your happiness. It is your own thoughts. They prevent you from being perfectly happy in the present moment. They are at the root of everything: your actions, reactions, emotions, judgements, the principles you have set yourself and the ideas that you cherish.

In order to rectify these situations you do not have to deal with them one at a time or even altogether. What is the point in taking rubbish out of a bin bit by bit if you want to empty it? Piece by piece or even by the dozen, it makes no difference. It suffices to take the entire back out the bin. The bin bag contains everything you want to get rid of, and this garbage bag is equivalent to the thoughts that drive all our actions and reactions, that produce our emotions, judgements, prejudices and that set out the principles by which we operate.

There are several methods and so-called spiritual paths which offer different ways of purifying the mind by working on thought processes. One is able to work directly on the foundational level which is the stage concerning the creation of thought. This is not an easy thing to do for everyone, it is difficult. One can also work on the following level which concerns emotion generated by thoughts. I propose using dreams as detectors of emotion which in turn detect foundational or original thoughts. No matter which stage you choose to work on, moving forward is the main thing: 'little by little, the bird makes its nest'. One gradually reaches more subtle stages to work on, and this process continues on. Remember, moving forward is the main thing. Only God knows where you will land, that is not our concern.

Even if this book did not manage to convince you, I at least know it works. What I have spoken of here works and I am the first to witness it: gaining more and more peace of mind, freedom, and self-confidence as well as gaining a greater understanding of the world and thinking up less essential questions to find answers to, having fewer emotions and dreams whilst the unique feeling of peace grows within me. For a long time I made a note of my dreams and analysed them and also sought help from a variety of therapists, but none of them helped me however qualified they were with their symbols and theories. It was Muni, a simple wise man who is known to no one who one day said something to me so simple yet full of wisdom: 'a dream is nothing other than the manifestation of the things you have had bad experiences of in the hours beforehand'.

My entire dream world made sense after that, and I transformed myself into my own dream interpreter.

If you are interested in the extraordinary adventures dreams can offer, then you will not even have to read this book because you would have dispensed with it from the first chapter. But if it is peace of heart in the depths of your soul that speaks to you, then there is a treasure within these pages that you can take and experiment with for yourself. If you put the few exercises I have presented to you into practise you will see the results. If not, then come and see me.

This book does not deal with the catechisms of the Catholic Church with its dogmas that you simply have to believe in if you want to be saved. Instead I am offering you a process to follow and verify yourself, just as scientists do. If you are looking for a method to interpret your dreams, at least commit yourself to it using a veritable technique. Not one that has limits and will go in circles about the dream world and its symbolisms. Do not use such a limited method that allows you to interpret some dreams whilst many others remain unclear. Instead, commit yourself to a genuine method that gives you a clear understanding of every dream no matter what kind it is or how many there are. And finally, you will dream less and less.

BIBLIOGRAPHY

-Thomas More ou la conscience d'un saint – Walter Nigg, 1979
-Les grandes familles de mots – Jean-Claude ROLLAND, 2016
-Le Rêve, Histoire et significations – Catherine Maillard, 2003
-L'interprétation des rêves – Sigmund Freud, 1899
-Essais sur l'expérience libératrice – Roger Godel, 1952
-À la recherche du soi (Tome 1-4) – Arnaud Desjardins, 1974
-Approches à la méditations – Arnaud Desjardins, 1989
-Langues inventées : Tolkien et les langues de la Terre du Milieu – Camille Gondral, 2018

ONLINE SOURCES

-Google
-Wikipedia
-Perrine Ruby, Chercheur en neuroscience cognitive, INSERM , « Pourquoi le cerveau se souvient-il de nos rêves ? » – communiqué de presse vidéo
-L'art de diriger ses rêves – Stephen LaBerge
-Les fans de Star Wars forment-ils la plus grande communauté de marque du monde ? - Article de Jolhane Leite, LinkedIN

INSPIRED BY THE TEACHINGS

-Muni
-Arnaud Desjardins
-Robert Scheinfeld

Meet me on...

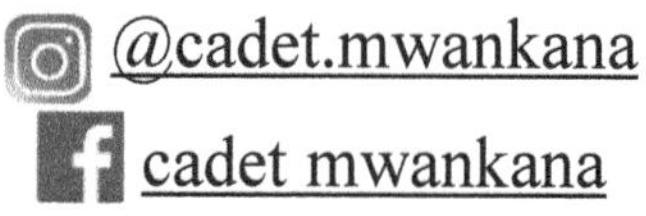

www.ingramcontent.com/pod-product-compliance
Ingram Content Group UK Ltd.
Pitfield, Milton Keynes, MK11 3LW, UK
UKHW021656190726
13853UKWH00001B/307